Independent Schools
Examinations Board

MIXED MATHS EXERCISES

Year 7

Andrew Jeffrey

© Independent Schools Examinations Board
Jordan House, Christchurch Road, New Milton BH25 6QJ

ISBN 0 903627 04 3

Printed in Great Britain
by Stephen Austin and Sons Limited, Hertford

INTRODUCTION

I hope that pupils will enjoy and benefit from using these mathematics exercises.

A careful glance through the exercises will reveal that new topics are constantly being introduced, and, in a gradual manner wherever possible. Nevertheless, it is always a good idea to look ahead in order to pre-empt any difficulties.

Andrew Jeffrey

1. Work out

    (i) 23 × 6   (ii) 230 × 6   (iii) 2.3 × 6   (iv) 2.3 × 60

2. Change these fractions into decimals.

    (i) $\frac{1}{2}$ (ii) $\frac{3}{4}$ (iii) $\frac{1}{10}$ (iv) $\frac{2}{5}$

3. What is the area of this rectangle?

    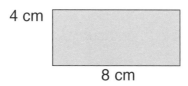

    4 cm

    8 cm

4. I think of a number, double it, and add 7
    The answer is 31
    Which number did I think of?

5. The letter x stands for the number 6
    What would be the value of $3x + 2$?

6. FLYTANIC is a film about an insect which drowns.
    The film starts at 9:45 pm and finishes at 11:20 pm.
    How long is it?

7.   (i) Draw a triangle with all the sides 6 cm long.

     (ii) Label on your diagram the size of one of the angles.

8. Work out

    (i) $\frac{3}{4}$ of 100   (ii) $\frac{4}{5}$ of 100

9. On Friday afternoon the temperature was 12 degrees Celsius.
    That night it dropped by 15 degrees.
    What was the night-time temperature?

BRAINBOX QUESTION
At a meeting of the Rottingdean Polite Society, all 10 people shake everyone else's hand once.
How many handshakes are there?

1. Change these percentages into fractions **in their lowest terms**.

    (i) 40%   (ii) 24%   (iii) 20%   (iv) $37\frac{1}{2}\%$

2. Change these fractions into percentages.

    (i) $\frac{1}{5}$ (ii) $\frac{3}{5}$ (iii) $\frac{6}{8}$

3. Change these decimals into percentages.

    (i) 0.03   (ii) 0.3   (iii) 0.775

4. I think of a number, treble it, and subtract 9
    The answer is 15
    Which number did I think of?

5. The letter x stands for the number 6
    What would be the value of $5x + 4$?

6. Angie and Brian are twins.
    On their birthday, their Mum makes them a cake.
    Angie eats $\frac{3}{5}$ of it.
    What **percentage** is left for Brian?

7. (i) Draw a right angle, with one line 3 cm long and the other line 4 cm long.
        Label the lengths.

    (ii) Join the other ends of the lines to make a triangle. Measure and label the
        third side.

8. Work out

    (i) $\frac{3}{4} + 0.9$ (ii) $\frac{4}{5}$ of £80

9. I roll two dice and add the scores together.
    How many different totals could I get?

BRAINBOX QUESTION
Two teachers multiply their ages together and arrive at a total of 999
How old are they?
(Sensible whole-number answers only!)

1. Change these percentages into fractions **in their lowest terms**.

   (i)   25%   (ii)   65%   (iii)   80%

2. Change these fractions into decimals.

   (i) $\dfrac{3}{10}$ (ii) $\dfrac{8}{20}$ (iii) $\dfrac{18}{25}$

3. If $x = 6$, $y = 7$ and $z = {}^-2$, calculate the value of

   (i) $x + y + z$ (ii) xy (iii) $3y - z$ (iv) $y(x + z)$

4. Larry eats $\frac{1}{2}$ of a packet of sweets, Curly eats 15% of the sweets, and Mo eats one fifth of the sweets.

   If there were 200 sweets to begin with, how many sweets are left in the packet?

5. If $3t - 6 = 18$, work out which number t stands for.

6. Three girls ran the 100 m in 12 s, 15 s, and 24 s respectively.

   What was their average time for the race?

7. Find

   (i)   10% of £50   (ii)   30% of 800 kg

8. Which number is exactly halfway between 1.5 and 3?

BRAINBOX QUESTION

I am thinking of a two-digit number.
It has exactly 3 factors.
Its second digit is 3 more than its first digit.
What is my number?
(Hint: make a short list of possibilities.)

1. Change these percentages into fractions **in their lowest terms.**

    (i) 30%   (ii) 4%   (iii) 90%   (iv) $12\frac{1}{2}\%$

2. Change these fractions into percentages.

    (i) $\frac{1}{10}$ (ii) $\frac{2}{5}$ (iii) $\frac{3}{8}$

3. Change these decimals into percentages.

    (i) 0.6   (ii) 0.09   (iii) 0.74

4. Simplify the following expressions by collecting like terms:

    (i) $3t - 5t$ (ii) $^-5t - {}^-3t$ (iii) $4p + 2q + 3p - 5q$

5. If $30 - 2q = 16$, what number does q stand for?

6.  Ray and Ruth are twins.

    On their birthday, their mum makes them a 1 kg cake.

    If Ray eats $\frac{2}{5}$ of it, and Ruth eats half of the remainder, what mass of cake is left?

    (Clue: how many grams in a kilogram?)

7. Evaluate (work out) the following using a number line:

    (i) $^-3 + 5$ (ii) $2 - 3 - {}^-6$ (iii) $^-4 - 2 + {}^-5$

8. What do you get if you add a half to a third?

BRAINBOX QUESTION
I have two red cards, a blue card and a green card, which must be laid in a horizontal row.
How many **different** colour combinations could this produce?
(*e.g. red, blue, red, green, etc.*)

1. Change these percentages into fractions **in their lowest terms.**

    (i) 20%   (ii) 8%   (iii) 70%   (iv) $37\frac{1}{2}$%

2. Change these fractions into percentages.

    (i) $\frac{4}{10}$ (ii) $\frac{20}{50}$ (iii) $\frac{30}{40}$

3. Change these decimals into percentages.

    (i) 0.7   (ii) 0.07   (iii) 1.5

4. Simplify the following expressions by collecting like terms:

    (i) $3t + 5t$ (ii) $^-5t - ^-9t$ (iii) $4p + 3q - 3p - 5q$

5. If $3x + 17 = 29$, what number does x stand for?

6. Add 3 hundreds, 8 hundredths, 5 tens, 2 tenths, and 26.83

7. Evaluate (work out) the following using a number line:

    (i) $^-3 + 5 - 4$ (ii) $2 - 5 - ^-6$ (iii) $^-4 - 2 + ^-5$

8. What do you get if you add a half to two thirds?

BRAINBOX QUESTION
This is a puzzle about two wealthy women.
If one owns five yachts and 2 million pounds, and the other owns three yachts and
5 million pounds, and these two fortunes are considered to be worth exactly the
same, can you work out the value of a yacht?
(You may assume that all the yachts are identical.)

1.   What percentage of the large rectangle is shaded?
     *(Hint: find out what **fraction** is shaded.)*

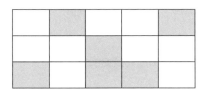

2.   Simplify these expressions.

     (i) $3t + 8t - 2t$ (ii) $3q \times q$

3.   Solve these equations by doing the same thing to both sides of each.

     (i) $2x + 7 = 11$ (ii) $5t - 4 = 31$

4.   Solve this equation by gradually taking things away from both sides.

     $$3y + 78 = 7y + 26$$

     (Show all your working.)

5.   Copy out and complete this equivalence table.

fraction	decimal	percentage
$\frac{2}{5}$		
	0.15	
		12

6.   If $a = 4$, $b = \frac{1}{2}$ and $c =~^-3$, evaluate

     (i) $a - b + c$ (ii) $a + b - c$ (iii) $7a(b - c)$

7.   Evaluate (work out) the following:

     (i) $^-6 + 15 - 4$ (ii) $102 - 105 - ^-106$ (iii) $^-4.5 - 2.5 + ^-5$

8.   Moses and Joshua share a loaf of bread.
     Moses eats one third of the loaf, and Joshua eats five twelfths of the loaf.
     What fraction of the loaf remains?

BRAINBOX QUESTION

The children at St Oddbins play tennis and hockey.
13 children play neither game.
$\frac{3}{4}$ of the children play both tennis and hockey, and 180 play hockey.
Altogether there are 200 children at the school.
How many play just tennis?

1. Solve the equations, showing each stage clearly.

   (i) $3q - 7 = q - 5$ (ii) $2w + 5 = 5w - 25$

2. John scores 11 out of 20 in his homework. What is his percentage?

3. Change these decimals into fractions **in their lowest terms**.

   (i) 0.5   (ii) 0.4   (iii) 0.08   (iv) 0.28

4.   (i) Draw axes in the first quadrant from 0 to 5

      (ii) Plot the points A (0,1) B (3,1) and C (5,3)

      (iii) $ABCD$ is a parallelogram. Find and label the point D.

      (iv) Join the points to make the parallelogram.

5. Vashti has sharpened her pencils. Their lengths, measured in centimetres, are

13.6	6.8	8.9	10.8
11.0	11.3	12.9	9.4
13.2	14.2	11.6	10.5

   (i) Copy out and complete this tally chart.

length (cm)	tally	frequency
6 – 7.99		
8 – 9.99		
10 – 11.99		
12 – 13.99		
14 – 15.99		

   (ii) What is the **modal** range of lengths?

BRAINBOX QUESTION

A computer company is offering a special deal to customers who buy four computers; 40% off the first machine, 30% off the second machine, 20% off the third, and 10% off the last.

If the **original** prices (in order) of the four computers were £1100, £900, £1500 and £2100, how much change would I receive from £4000?

1. Solve these equations.

    (i) $8p - 6 = 3p + 9$ (ii) $4y + 6 = 7y - 12$

2. Louise receives 36 out of a possible 40 marks in a science test.
    What is her percentage?

3. Change these decimals into fractions **in their lowest terms**.

    (i)   0.2   (ii)   0.25   (iii)   0.24   (iv)   1.2

4. (i)   Draw axes in the first quadrant from 0 to 5

    (ii)   Plot the points A (1,1) B (4,0) and C (5,3)

    (iii) $ABCD$ is a square. Find and label the point D.

    (iv)   Join the points to make the square.

5. Here are the heights of 15 children in Mr Greek's class, measured in metres.

1.30	1.45	1.54	1.31	1.66
1.29	1.43	1.36	1.09	1.44
1.47	1.53	1.32	1.60	1.48

    (i)   Copy and complete this tally chart and frequency table.

height (metres)	tally	frequency
1.00 – 1.09		
1.10 – 1.19		
1.20 – 1.29		
1.30 – 1.39		
1.40 – 1.49		
1.50 – 1.59		
1.60 – 1.69		

    (ii)   Draw a frequency diagram, using the data from your table.

    (iii)   What was the modal range of heights?

BRAINBOX QUESTION

Alison scores 3 more marks than Andrew in an ICT test.
Her **percentage** score is 15% higher than Andrew's.
How many marks were available in the test altogether?
(The answer 100% is not allowed!)

1. Calculate 327 × 64

2. Find $\frac{1}{4}$ of 180 kg.

3. What is 50% of £6?

4. What is the sum of $3\frac{1}{2}$ and 0.7?

5. What are the next two numbers in this sequence?

    5.3   8.2   11.1   14.0   ...   ...

6. Find 3 numbers which multiply together to make 18

7. If $t = 3$, what is $2t - 1$?

8. Simplify $5x + 2 - 2x + 7$

9. Solve $3a - 4 = 11$

10. What is the **mean** (average) of **2**, **2**, **6** and **10**?

11. What is the probability that an unbiased 6-sided die rolled at random will show a five?

12. A recipe for 4 people needs 6 eggs. How many eggs would be needed for 12 people?

13. Write the number 299 to the nearest hundred.

14. Find the missing angle.

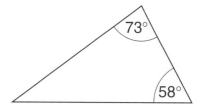

15. I walk from home to the park in a straight line, heading SW.
    In which direction must I walk to return home?

16. Multiply out $3(t + 4)$

17. The number 60 has 12 factors.

    (i) What are they?

    (ii) How many of them are prime?

BRAINBOX QUESTION

I am thinking of a two-digit number.
4 is a factor of my number, but 3 and 5 are not.
The second digit is 1 less than the first digit.
What is my number?
How many solutions are there?

1. Calculate 354 × 27

2. Find $\frac{3}{4}$ of 300 km.

3. What is 25% of £5?

4. What is the sum of $5\frac{1}{2}$ and 2.7?

5. What are the next two numbers in this sequence?

0.5   0.9   1.3   1.7   ...   ...

6. Express 24 as a product of prime factors.

7. If $t = 3$, what is $4t - 4$?

8. Simplify the expression $6x - 2 - 2x + 7$

9. Solve the equation $2q + 7 = 15$

10. What is the **mean** (average) of 2, 3, 4 and 7?

11. What is the probability that an unbiased 6-sided die rolled at random will show a three?

12. Calculate the difference between the furthest distance and the shortest distance in the following list: 3.1 cm, 2.6 cm, 65 mm, 29 mm, 5 cm.
    *(This number is called the **range** of the data.)*

13. Write the number 219 to 1 significant figure.

14. Find the missing angle (marked θ).

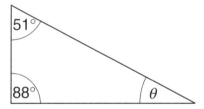

15. I walk from home to the park in a straight line, heading SE.
    In which direction must I walk to return home?

16. What is the area of a rectangle measuring 3.5 cm by 4 cm?

17. Multiply out $3(2q + 3)$

BRAINBOX QUESTION

I start from a mystery set of co-ordinates.
I travel 5 units right, 4 units down, 3 units left, and 2 units up.
My final co-ordinates are (3,0).
What are the co-ordinates of my starting point?

1. Calculate 3.54 × 2.7 *(show working)*

2. Find $\frac{2}{3}$ of 180

3. What is 15% of 800 metres?

4. What is the sum of $3\frac{1}{4}$ and 2.8?

5. Express 210 as the product of prime factors.

6. If $a = 2$ and $b = \frac{1}{2}$, find the value of $a^2 + 3b$.

7. Simplify $5 - 8x - 3 + 12 - 4x$.

8. Solve the equation $5 + 3x = 14$

9. Which number appears most often in the following list?

   2, 5, 7, 6, 3, 8, 4, 4, 5, 2, 6, 9, 11, 5, 3

   *(This number is known as the **mode**.)*

10. Write the number 3.7602 correct to 2 significant figures.

11. What is the area of a right-angled triangle whose base is 4 cm and whose height is 3 cm?

12. Factorise the expression $25x + 15y$.

13. The ages of two girls are in the ratio 3:1

    If the younger girl is 5, what is the age of the older girl?

14. What is the probability that if a form captain is chosen at random from your class, it is you?

15. How many 1 cm cubes could fit in this box?

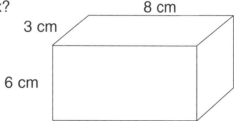

BRAINBOX QUESTION

I start from a mystery set of co-ordinates.
I travel 3 units right, 3 units down, 1 unit left, and 2 more units down.
My final co-ordinates are (⁻2,⁻2).
What are the co-ordinates of my starting point?

1. Calculate 9.2×0.04

2. $\frac{5}{8}$ of a number is 30   What is the number?

3. Reduce the number 565 by 40%

4. Find the value of $1\frac{5}{8} + 2\frac{1}{2}$

5. What are the next two numbers in this sequence?

    0.1   0.2   0.4   0.8   ...   ...

6. What is the area of this triangle?

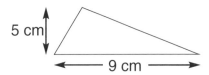

7. Simplify $3t + 7 - 5t - 3t + 8$

8. Solve the equation $3p - 6 = p + 20$

9. If $a = 3$ and $b = {}^-2$, what is the value of $a^2 - b^2$?

10. Factorise $24x^2 + 30xt$.

11. What is the **median** of the following data?

    3, 2, 3, 6, 5, 2, 7, 1, 3, 8, 7, 4, 9, 10, 6, 3

12. Express 420 as the product of prime factors.

13. Bill and Ted share some money in the ratio 7:4
    If Bill has £6 more than Ted, how much money do they have altogether?

14. How many eighths are there in 4.5?

15. Estimate, to one significant figure, (*do not calculate*) the answer to $\dfrac{48 \times 2.3}{19.9 \div 3.9}$

BRAINBOX QUESTION
Try to find the length and width of the rectangle which has a perimeter of 34 cm and an area of 72 cm^2.

1. Calculate 9.2×1.04 *(show working)*.

2. $\frac{5}{8}$ of a number is 12.5   What is the number?

3. Reduce the number 560 by 35%

4. Find the value of $2\frac{5}{8} + 1\frac{1}{2}$

5. Find the next two numbers in this sequence.

   1.2   1.5   2.1   3.0   ...   ...

6. Calculate *(showing all your working)* the area of this triangle.

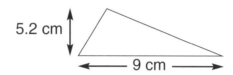

7. Simplify $3t + 7(t + 4)$

8. Solve the equation $3p - 6 = p - 20$

9. If $a = \frac{1}{2}$ and $b = {}^-2$, what is the value of $a^2 - b^2$?

10. Factorise $24bx^2 + 36xt$.

11. Find the **range** of the following data:

    3,   2,   3,   6,   5,   2,   7,   1,   3,   8,   7,   4,   9,   10,   6

12. Express 232 as the product of prime factors.

13. How many sixths are there in 4.5?

14. Calculate the size of angle θ

BRAINBOX QUESTION
The three sides of a triangle are in the ratio 2:3:5 and its perimeter (i.e. the sum of all three sides) is 60 cm. Can you work out all three lengths?

1. Calculate 0.27×3.6

2. $\frac{5}{8}$ of a number is 20   What is the number?

3. Increase the number 480 by 45%

4. Find the value of $2\frac{1}{2} + \frac{5}{6}$

5. What is the area of this shape?

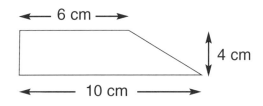

Hint: split the area into 2 pieces!

6. Simplify $5(x + 3) + 3(x + 2)$

7. Solve the equation $2p + 15 = 5p + 9$

8. If $a = \frac{1}{2}$, what is the value of $5a^2$?

9. Factorise $14at + 21xt$.

10. Find the **median** of the following data:

$$3, \ 2, \ 3, \ 6, \ 5, \ 2, \ 7, \ 1, \ 3, \ 8, \ 7, \ 4, \ 9, \ 10, \ 6$$

11. Express 91 as the product of prime factors.

12. What is $20 \div \frac{1}{4}$? *(All working must be shown.)*

13. Calculate the size of angle *CDB*.

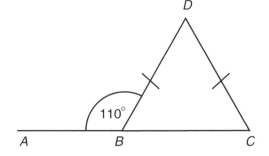

BRAINBOX QUESTION

The three sides of a triangle are in the ratio 2:3:5, and the **range** of the lengths is 15 cm. Can you work out all three lengths?

1. **Without using a calculator**, simplify and evaluate $\dfrac{1.4 \times 10}{0.28 \times 100}$

2. Change these mixed numbers into improper fractions.

   (i) $2\frac{1}{3}$ (ii) $4\frac{3}{4}$

3. Change these improper fractions into mixed numbers.

   (i) $\frac{7}{4}$ (ii) $\frac{7}{3}$

4. Multiply $2\frac{1}{2}$ by $\frac{3}{10}$

5. Simplify $3x + 5 - 2x - 5$

6. Solve the equation $4(x + 2) = 20$

7. If $a = 3$, $b = 4$ and $c = {}^-2$, find the value of

   (i) $3a + 2b$ (ii) $3b + 3c$ (iii) $ab - c$

8. 30% of a number is 21
   What is the number?

9.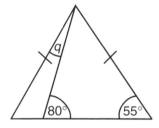

   What is the size of
   angle q?

   *(Hint: you need to find
   some other angles first.)*

10. Factorise $15x^2 + 10x$.

11. Add $\frac{2}{3}$ to $3\frac{1}{2}$ *(no calculators; show working)*

12. Write down a square number which is even and has 5 as a factor.

13. Find a pair of prime numbers which add up to 36

14. Mike is x years old.
    Oscar is 2 years older than Mike.
    Write down an **expression, in terms of x**, for Oscar's age.

15. Charlie is twice Oscar's age.
    Find **an expression** for Charlie's age.

BRAINBOX QUESTION

What year will it be one million seconds from today? *(Calculators are permitted!)*

1. **Without using a calculator**, simplify and evaluate $\dfrac{0.27 \times 100}{360 \div 10}$

2. Change these mixed numbers into improper fractions.

   (i) $5\frac{1}{3}$ (ii) $11\frac{3}{4}$

3. Change these improper fractions into mixed numbers.

   (i) $\frac{23}{4}$ (ii) $\frac{79}{3}$

4. Multiply $2\frac{1}{2}$ by $\frac{3}{4}$

5. Simplify $3x + 5 + 2(2x - 4)$

6. Solve the equation $4(x + 2) = 20 + x$.

7. If $a = 3$, $b = \dfrac{1}{2}$ and $c = {}^-2$, find the value of

   (i) $3a + 2b$ (ii) $3(b + c)$ (iii) $ab - c$

8. 35% of a number is 14
   What is the number?

9. A square has a perimeter of 30 cm.
   What is its area?

10. Factorise $15x^2 + 10x + 5xy$.

11. Add $\frac{2}{3}$ to $3\frac{1}{2}$ *(no calculators; show working)*

12. Write down the 10th prime number.

13. Find a pair of prime numbers which add up to 40

14. Reuben has x sweets.
    Simeon has 3 more than Reuben.
    Levi has twice as many as Simeon.
    Write down and simplify an **expression** for the number of sweets they have altogether.

15. If the 3 boys from question 14 have 29 sweets altogether, form and solve an equation to find how many sweets each boy has.

BRAINBOX QUESTION

How many different ways of making 40 are there by adding 2 prime numbers together?

1. A pie chart displays data about the colour of people's hair. If the sector showing the seven people with purple hair measures 140°, how many people were surveyed altogether?

2.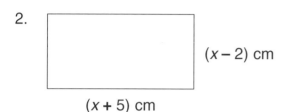

   $(x - 2)$ cm   Write down and simplify *(by collecting like terms)* an expression for the perimeter of the rectangle.

   $(x + 5)$ cm

3. What is the 100th number in this sequence? (*Do not write 100 terms!*)

   3   7   11   15   19   ...

4. Factorise $12qt + 15q^2 + 12q^3t$.

5. A jacket was included in a sale offering 20% off, at a reduced price of £12
   What was the original price?

6. Calculate the value of $3\frac{1}{2} \times 2\frac{1}{7}$ *(Do not use a calculator; you must show working.)*

7. Solve the equations

   (i) $4(x - 3) = 5(3 - x)$ (ii) $5 - 7x = 19 + 7x$

8. Find the area of this trapezium.

   (Hint: it may help you to do it in sections.)

   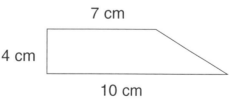

   7 cm

   4 cm

   10 cm

9. Express 400 as the product of prime factors.

BRAINBOX QUESTION

A cricketer's batting average is calculated by dividing the total number of runs he has scored by the total number of times he has been out.
David's batting average (after four innings) was 50.
After his fifth innings, his average went down to 44. How many runs did he score in the fifth innings? (*You may assume that he was out each time he batted.*)

1. A pie chart displays data about a variety of interesting people.

    If the sector showing the six people with wooden legs is a right angle, how many people were surveyed altogether?

2.

    $(x-1)$ cm

    $(x+8)$ cm

    The perimeter of the rectangle is 50 cm.

    Form and solve an equation to find x.

3. What is the 50th number in this sequence? *(Do not write out 50 terms!)*

    15   12   9   6   3   0   ...

4. Factorise $12qt + 18q^2 + 12\,q$.

5. What is the circumference of this circle? *(Give your answer correct to 1 decimal place.)*

    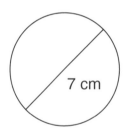

    7 cm

6. Calculate the value of $4\frac{1}{2} \times 2\frac{1}{6}$ *(Do not use a calculator; you **must** show working.)*

7. Solve the equations

    (i) $4\left(\frac{x}{3}\right) = 16$ (ii) $5 + \frac{x}{2} = 2$

8. Without a calculator, find the value of

    $$\frac{1.4 \times 100}{3.5 \times 10}$$

BRAINBOX QUESTION

Using any **two** of the numbers 4, 6, and 8 and **one** of the operations $+$, $-$, $\times$, $\div$, which of the five numbers $^-2$, $\frac{2}{3}$, 1.5, 16, 48 is it **not** possible to make?

Calculators are permitted only in question 3.

1. Calculate   (i) 3.29×2.4 (ii) $350 \div 0.7$

2. Find the 100th term in this sequence $^-2$ 4   10   16   ...

3. What is the area of this circle, correct to 1 decimal place?

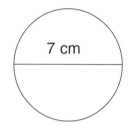

7 cm

4. Find $\frac{3}{4}$ of $(2\frac{1}{2} + 1\frac{1}{3})$

5. After an increase of 10%, Alison's wages go up to £198 per week.

   How much was she paid before the increase?

6. If $a = 3$, $b = {}^-2$ and $c = 0.5$, calculate

   (i) abc (ii) $\dfrac{a+b}{2c}$

7. Multiply out and collect like terms

   $$7(t + 4) + 3(2t - 5)$$

8. Solve these equations.

   (i) $3q - 4 = 6 - q$ (ii) $\dfrac{5p}{3} = 10$

9. A bag contains 3 red, 4 yellow and 2 green balls.

   If I remove a ball at random, what is the probability that

   (i)   the ball is red   (ii)   the ball is **not** yellow?

10. Which of these expressions has the largest value?

      $3 \times 9 + 9$ $9 + 3 \times 9$ $3 + 9 \times 9$ $9 \times 3 + 9$ $3 + 9 \times 3$

BRAINBOX QUESTION

The area of a rectangle is 54 cm², and its perimeter is 30 cm. Find the length and the width of the rectangle.

Calculators are permitted only in question 3.

1. Express these numbers as fractions **in their lowest terms**.

    (i) 0.475 (ii) 80%

2. Find the 40th term in this sequence:

    10 16 22 28 ...

    (Hint: find an expression for the nth term; then let n = 40)

3. What is the area of a semi-circle whose radius is 5 cm?

4. Find $\frac{2}{3}$ of $(3\frac{1}{2} + 2\frac{2}{3})$

5. After an increase of 10%, Alison's wages go up to £253 per week. How much was she paid before the increase?

6. Factorise fully

    (i) $5a + 10ab + 50a^2$ (ii) $3pq + 39qw$

7. Multiply out and collect like terms

    $$7(t + 4) - 3(2t - 5)$$

8. Solve these equations.

    (i) $3f - 8 = 6 + f$ (ii) $\frac{4f}{5} = 8$

9. A bag contains 20 balls, numbered from 1 to 20
    If the set P = {prime numbers}, and the set T = {two digit numbers}, draw a Venn diagram showing where each ball goes.
    Hence or otherwise find the probability that a ball picked at random **does** have two digits but is not prime.

10. Express 300 as the product of prime factors.

BRAINBOX QUESTION

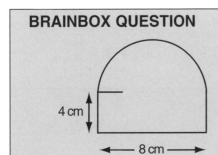

If the base of this shape is 8 cm long, and the length of each straight section of vertical wall is 4 cm, what is the area of the whole shape?

1. **Without using a calculator**, work out

    (i)   600 ÷ 0.3   (ii)   3.7 × 10 + 4.9 × 100

2. Find the area and perimeter of this shape.

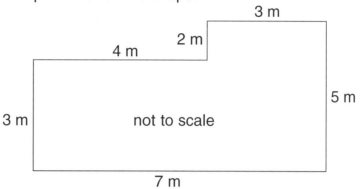

3. Jo's salary was £18 000

   How much would she earn after a 5% rise?

4. Here are the history and science examination marks of 10 people.

history	52	40	81	63	27	42	55	90	66	66
science	40	24	60	44	20	40	30	80	40	55

    (i) Using a scale of 1 cm to 10 marks, draw a scattergraph to display this information.

    (ii) On your diagram, draw a line of best fit.

5.   (i) From the data in question 4, what, if any, correlation was there?

     (ii) Gerry scored 70 in history. What might she score in science?

6. Find $(\frac{2}{3} + \frac{4}{5}) \times 1\frac{7}{8}$

7. Solve   (i) $32 - 3p = 20$ (ii) $4(3 + y) = 20$

8. Simplify   (i) $3(3 + p) - 2(4 + p)$ (ii) $a + a - a$

9. Find the exterior and interior angles of a regular pentagon.

10. Estimate to 1 significant figure $\dfrac{27 \times 42}{8.3}$

BRAINBOX QUESTION
What is the sum of the interior angles of a regular heptagon?

1.   **Without using a calculator**, work out

   (i) $3462 \div 9$ (ii) $3462 \div 0.9$

2.   Find the value of   (i) $\frac{4}{5} - \frac{5}{8}$ (ii) $\frac{2}{7} \div \frac{2}{10}$

3.   The population of Great Britain on 1st January 1999 was estimated by statisticians to be fifty-eight million.
   If it increases by 1% per annum, estimate the size of the population on 1st January 2000

4.   The times taken by 15 children to run 200 m are given below, accurate to the nearest second.

25	36	41	31	28
30	31	34	39	42
26	39	24	33	45

   (i) Find the **mean** time, to the nearest second.

   (ii) Copy out and complete this table.

time	tally	frequency
20 – 24		
25 – 29		
30 – 34		
35 – 39		
40 – 45		

   (iii) What is the **median** time?

   (iv) What is the **modal** group?

5.   Solve the equations

   (i) $12 - 3p = 8$ (ii) $5(3 + y) = 12$

6.   Simplify the following expressions:

   (i) $2(5 - a) + 3(a - 5)$ (ii) $t \times t \div t$

7.   If $p = 2$, $q = {}^-3$ and $r = 3$, evaluate   (i) pqr (ii) $\dfrac{pr}{q}$

8.   Stephanie has 40 sweets.
   She eats 25% of them, then gives 20% of the remainder to her sister.
   How many does she have left?

BRAINBOX QUESTION

Use your answer to question 8 to show why $0.8 \times 0.75 \times 40 = 24$

1. **Without using a calculator**, work out   (i)   three fifths of 800   (ii) $284.2 \div 0.07$

2. Find the value of   (i) $2\frac{5}{8} - \frac{4}{5}$ (ii) $\frac{12}{7} \div \frac{3}{10}$

3. 70% of the children in a school want England to win the World Cup.
   There are 27 children who do **not** want England to win.
   How many children are there altogether?

4. In the St Oddbins gardening competition, the children check to see who has grown
   the tallest sunflower. The results are shown below.

   height measurements in cm to the nearest cm

114	113	124	144	151	109	133	136	120	119
101	136	127	112	115	164	133	124	111	138

   (i) Copy and complete the table below, extending it as necessary.

height	tally	frequency
100 – 109		
110 – 119		
120 – 129		
130 – 139		
140 – 149		
150 – 159		

   (ii) What is the modal group?

   (iii) What is the median height?

   (iv) What is the range of the data?

5. Draw a pie chart to show the above information.

6. Solve the inequalities

   (i) $3p + 1 < 10$ (ii) $4q - 5 > 13$

7. Simplify the following expressions:

   (i) $3(5 - 2a) + 3(2a - 5)$ (ii) $t \times t \times t \div t$

8. If $p = 5$, $q = {}^-2$ and $r = {}^-3$, evaluate   (i) pqr (ii) $\dfrac{pr}{q}$

BRAINBOX QUESTION
Which special number is the same as the sum and the product of all its factors?
(other than itself, of course!)

1.   Work out

     (i) 2.56 × 7   (ii) 25.6 × 0.27

2.   Solve these equations.

     (i) $3(w + 2) = 7w - 6$ (ii) $2(q - 2) = 10$

3.   Find the nth term of this sequence.

                       5   7   9   11   ...

4.   If I throw a red die and a
     green die together, in how
     many ways could I score a
     total of **eleven**?

5.   What is the probability of scoring a total of **eleven** with two dice?

6.   A quick survey of the members of class 3Z revealed the following geographical
     origins:

     8 British 4 other European 5 Asian 1 American

     Draw and label a pie chart to show this data.

7.   (i) Writing down **all** the figures shown by your calculator, evaluate

$$\frac{23.6 \times 0.39}{87.2 - 3.89}$$

     (ii) Write your answer to part (i) to 1 significant figure.

     (iii) Write your answer to part (i) to 1 decimal place.

BRAINBOX QUESTION
A circle has a circumference of 100 cm.
What is its radius?

1. Evaluate

   (i)　$56 \div 0.8$　　　　(ii)　$5.6 \div 0.5$

2. Solve these equations.

   (i)　$4(w + 2) = 6 - 2w$　(ii)　$2(3 - q) = 10$

3. Find the nth term of this sequence.

   7　10　13　16　...

4.
   If I throw a red die and a green die together, in how many ways could I score a total of **ten**?

5. What is the probability of scoring a total of **ten** with two dice?

6. A quick survey of the members of Year 7 revealed the following favourite sports:

   25% rugby　　　**35% netball**　　　**22% swimming**　　　**18% others**

   Draw and label a pie chart to show this data.

7. (i) Writing down **all** the figures shown by your calculator, evaluate

   $$\frac{23.6 \times 0.39}{87.2 - 3.89}$$

   (ii) Write your answer to part (i) to 2 significant figures.

   (iii) Write your answer to part (i) to 2 decimal places.

BRAINBOX QUESTION
A circle has an area of 150 cm^2.
What is its radius?

1. Approximately how many kilometres is 10 miles?

2. George, Adam and Mahin form the front row of the St Oddbins rugby scrum.

    Adam has played in x matches this season.

    George has played in two more matches than Adam.

    (i) Write down an expression for the number of matches in which George has played.

    (ii) Mahin has played in one more match than George. Write down an expression for the number of matches in which Mahin has played.

3.
Isabelle has 6 seemingly identical keys.

Only two of the keys will open her padlock.

What is the probability that the first key Isabelle tries will open the lock?

(*Be careful to give your answer in its lowest terms.*)

4. (i) If 41 girls have 38 CDs each, **estimate** the total number of CDs that the girls own.

    (ii) Now **calculate exactly** the total number of CDs.

5. Multiply out these brackets.

    (i) $3(4p - 6)$ (ii) $5(2q - 7)$

6. Simplify these expressions.

    (i) $5t - 8 - 2t + 5$ (ii) $6x^2 \div 15x$

BRAINBOX QUESTION
If the area of a circle is 60 cm^2, what is its circumference?

1.   Approximately how many miles is 10 kilometres?

2.   (i)   Marvo the magician charges his clients according to the scale on the right.

     How much would he charge for 2 hours' work?

     (ii) The cost of a series of shows was £130

     For how many hours must Marvo have worked?

MARVO THE MAGICIAN! DETAILS OF FEES:

£40 basic charge, plus £30 per half-hour

3.   **Estimate** the answer to this calculation.

$$9.87 \times (51 \times 1.99)$$

4.

Jonno **always** has either jam, marmalade or chocolate spread on his toast at breakfast time.

The probability that he has marmalade is 0.4

The probability that he has jam is $\frac{1}{10}$

What is the probability that Jonno will choose chocolate spread next Tuesday?

5.   Multiply out these brackets.

     (i) $3w(w + 5)$ (ii) $x(x - 1)$

6.   Simplify these expressions.

     (i) $p - p - p$ (ii) $p \times p \times p$

BRAINBOX QUESTION

Norbert has £1000 to give to charity.

He gives away £1 on January 1, £2 on January 2, £4 on January 3, £8 on January 4, and so on.

On which date will he run out of money?

1.   Express the number 340 as the product of prime factors.

2.    The *WOBBLY INTERNET CAFE* charges each customer for using its internet computers, according to a simple formula:

$$c = 200 + 2n$$

where c is the total cost, in pence, and n is the number of minutes the customer is online.

   (i) How much would Rachael pay for 1 hour online time?

   (ii) Wilby is charged £3.90

   For how long was he online?

3.   What is the volume of this cube?

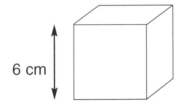

6 cm

4.   Draw an accurate net of a square-based pyramid.

5.   Solve these equations.

   (i) $3w + 2(w + 1) = 12 + w$ (ii) $\dfrac{4}{q} = 8$

6.   Simplify these expressions.

   (i) $p - (p - p)$ (ii) $p \times (p \times p)$

BRAINBOX QUESTION
Describe a possible method of calculating 49 × 80 **in your head!**

1. If $x = 3$, $y = 4$ and $z = {}^-2$, evaluate

    (i) xy (ii) $xy + z$ (iii) $x^2 - y^2 + z^2$

2. Find the sum of

    3 tenths,   **17 hundredths,** $\frac{1}{4}$

3. I jog for 15 minutes at 10 km/h, and then walk for 30 minutes at 4 km/h. How far do I travel altogether?

4. VAT is calculated to be $17\frac{1}{2}\%$ of an item's basic price. What would be the VAT for an item with a basic price of £300?

5. Nine children each choose a number between 1 and 20, and list them as follows:

12	**16**	**9**	**7**	**3**	**2**	**18**	**12**	**5**

    Find (i) the mean

        (ii) the mode

        (iii) the median, and

        (iv) the range.

6. Multiply out and simplify

    (i) $3(r - 3) + 2(5 + 2r)$ (ii) $6(p + 1) - 2(3 - p)$

7. Factorise fully

    (i) $q^3 + q^2$ (ii) $15w^2 + 20wp$

BRAINBOX QUESTION
I drive the school minibus in France.
A signpost tells me that my destination is 400 km away.
Approximately how long will it take me to get there driving at a steady 50 mph?
(Be careful with units!)

1. Find the area and circumference of a circle with diameter 15 cm.

2. *HEAP O'JUNK Car Rentals Ltd.* use the following formula to calculate the cost of hiring one of their cars for a fixed time:

    $$c = 75 + 30d$$

    where c is the total hire charge, and d is the number of days for which the car is required.

    (i) Calculate the total cost of hiring a car for one week.

    (ii) Calculate the cost of hiring a car for a fortnight.

    (iii) Adrian hired a car, and the total hire charge was £255

    Form and solve an equation in d to find out the number of days for which Adrian hired the car.

3. 8 of King Arthur's knights were Saxons, 5 were French and the others were both Cornishmen.

    Show this information in a pie chart.

4. The scroll shows a formula for calculating the area of any trapezium, given the height (h), and the lengths of the two parallel sides (t and b).

    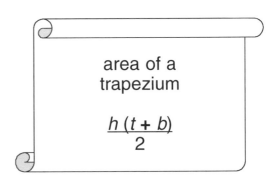

    area of a
    trapezium

    $$\frac{h\,(t+b)}{2}$$

    If $h = 3$ cm, $b = 4$ cm and $t = 5$ cm, calculate the area of the trapezium.

5. Write down all the prime numbers between 0 and 100

BRAINBOX QUESTION

Explain how, without any calculating aids, you could work out the answer to 6.5 × 2.8 + 3.5 × 2.8 **in your head**!

(It's very easy when you know how!)